Venta Icenorum

CAISTOR ST EDMUND
ROMAN TOWN

JOHN A. DAVIES
Chief Curator
Norfolk Museums and Archaeology Service

With illustrations by
SUE WHITE

*Age silver face-horse coin from Caistor
Scale 3:1*

Norfolk Archaeological Trust

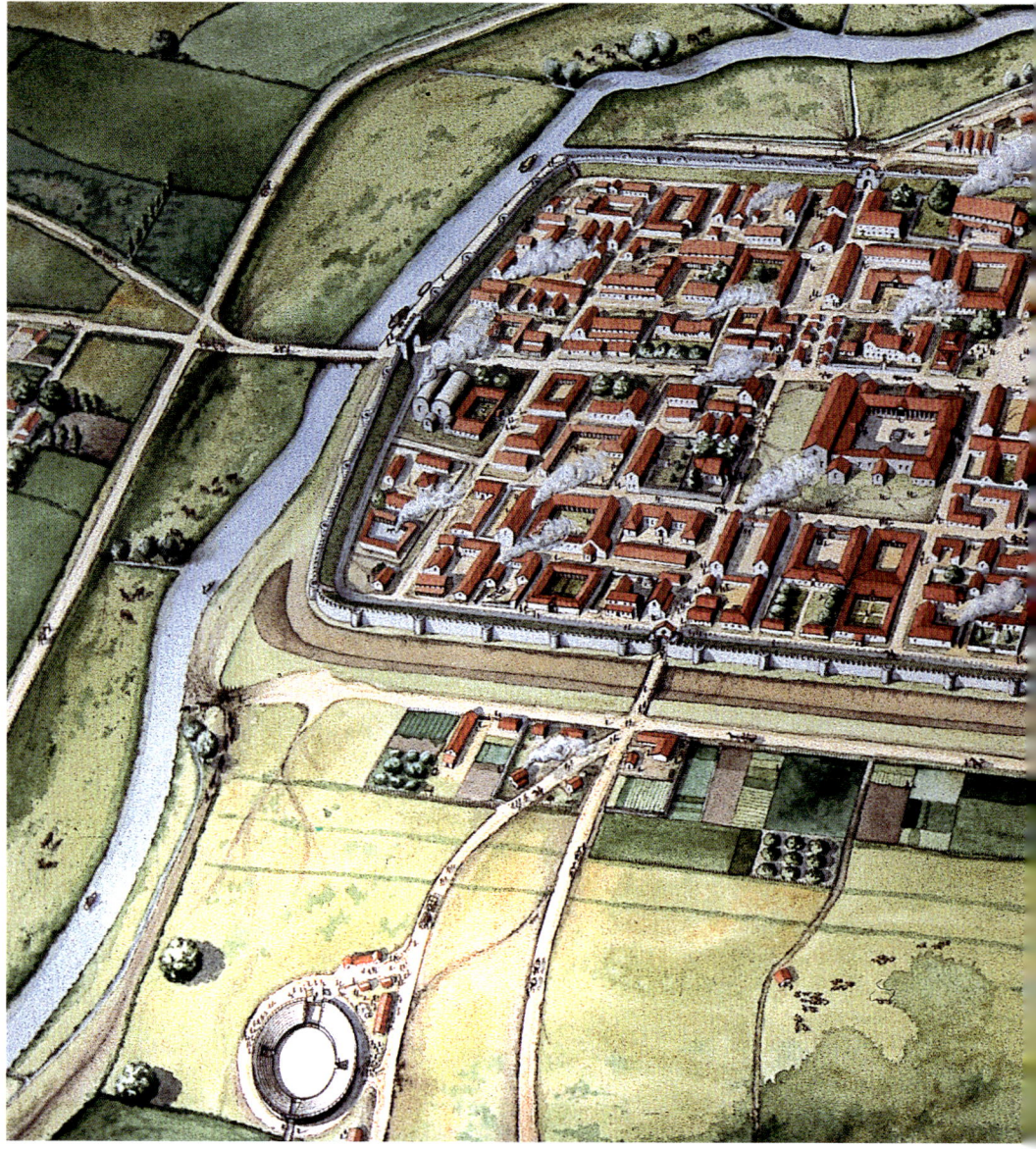

Contents

- 3 Introduction
- 4 Background
- 7 The earliest settlement in the Tas Valley
- 8 The Client Kingdom and its fall
- 10 Enter the Romans
- 12 Foundation of the Roman town
- 13 The early Roman town
- 17 Industry and trade
- 19 Everyday life in the town
- 21 Recreation
- 22 Religion and burials
- 23 The late Roman town
- 26 The end of the Roman town
- 27 The Church of St Edmund
- 29 The site within its landscape
  - *Tour of the site*
  - *Finds from the site*
  - *Further reading*

Introduction

At Caistor St. Edmund are the remains of a Roman town. Remarkable massive walls are a vivid reminder of the importance held by this once bustling and important settlement. Here is a site of both local and national importance. Originally known as *Venta Icenorum*, this was one of the regional capitals of Roman Britain and was the major town of northern East Anglia. It performed an administrative role and represented Roman authority. This was the biggest market centre for traded produce and was the main redistribution centre for goods travelling within and beyond the region. It was also a religious focus for the local countryside and provided entertainments, to which people from the surrounding area came on a regular basis. Today, *Venta Icenorum* offers a more tranquil location to visit. Within a peaceful country setting, it contrasts with its modern counterpart of Norwich, just 5 km to the north.

Venta Icenorum lies 5 km to the south of Norwich city centre, in the parish of Caistor St. Edmund, and just 800m south of the Norwich southern Bypass (A47T). There is a car park to the south of the site. It can be located on OS 1:50,000 sheet 134, TG230034.

The town in later Roman Britain

The north wall

Background

Venta Icenorum was the largest and most important Roman town in northern East Anglia. It was founded next to the River Tas, at a location within the modern parish of Caistor St. Edmund, during the 60s AD and was occupied until the end of Roman Britain. *Venta* was the administrative centre for the region inhabited by the Iceni tribe, whose territory covered modern Norfolk, the northern part of Suffolk and north-east Cambridgeshire. With Silchester, in Hampshire, and Wroxeter, in Shropshire, it is one of the few major Roman towns in Britain whose sites have never since been re-occupied. The remains of the Roman town have survived unaffected by later digging and building work, although there has been plough damage to the upper levels. Consequently, we have been left with a remarkably well-preserved ancient site for future study.

The period of Roman Britain lasted for over 350 years, which is the the equivalent of the period from the reign of King Charles I to the present day. There were obviously many changes during that time. Towns in Britain saw continual developments, the most visible of which at *Venta* was the construction of substantial defensive walls for the final 140 years or so of Roman occupation. The entire period saw

Aerial view, looking north, showing Roman streets

Aerial view, looking towards south-west

the growth of the town from its initial layout, through the construction of grand public buildings, its increasing prominence as a focus for trade, and the construction of the great defences to its final decline. This development and change will be described in the following pages.

Venta Icenorum is the Roman name, which means 'market place of the Iceni'. The Romans divided up lowland Britain into sixteen *civitates*, which were local government units, and were based very largely on the existing Iron Age tribal areas. From the second half of the first century to the early years of the fifth, *Venta* was the centre of Roman civil administration for the region, overseeing all local affairs. Such sites, known as *civitas* capitals, were the equivalent of today's county towns.

The name of *Venta Icenorum* is known from a Roman document called the Antonine Itinerary, which is a manuscript attributable to the early third century, describing 225 of the major roads of the Empire and listing places on them, and distances between them. *Venta* is listed in the British section as *Icinos* (on Route V) and *Venta Icinorum* (on Route IX). Ptolemy, a celebrated geographer writing in the second century AD, described *Venta* as the one noteworthy town among the Iceni.

Early interest in the site can be traced back to the time of Queen Elizabeth I. William Camden, who lived between 1551-1623, recognised that this was the site listed in the Antonine Itinerary. Camden took a particular interest in the remains and described their physical appearance. He stated, 'the faces of the four gates are still manifestly to be seen', as well as 'platforms of the houses and other buildings'. In the eighteenth century, John Kirkpatrick (who died in 1728) left a description of the visible remains as, 'monuments of a castle in it invironing fifty acres of ground, and ringbolts in the walls, whereto ships were fastened'. This is evidence for the presence of a Roman wharf, adjacent to the town's west gate. With regard to its function, Francis Blomefield, an antiquarian writing in about 1725, considered that Caistor was a station 'to guard the river Tas'.

Not everybody accepted Camden's view that Caistor was indeed *Venta Icenorum*. This subject continued to cause considerable debate among antiquarians. Blomefield considered North Elmham to be the most likely location for *Venta* and Spelman suggested that it was at Bergh Apton. Others favoured Norwich. However, writing in 1831, Samuel Woodward supported Camden's earlier conclusion that the site was indeed *Venta Icenorum*, and stated that this was, by then, a matter of universal acceptance.

During the later 19th century *Venta Icenorum* increasingly became the focus of antiquarian attention. There is an account by Reverend Hart which angrily described 'a shameful act of vandalism' in which flint bastions which were attached to the town wall were being demolished in order to repair local roads. Other debates at that time considered the role of the site and its function in relation to other well-preserved East Anglian Roman sites, such as the late Roman fort at Burgh Castle, which also had (and still has) impressive walls. Interest intensified in the early years of this century when the similar 'greenfield' site at Silchester, in Hampshire, was completely uncovered between 1890 and 1909.

With regard to the size and status of the site, Professor Haverfield, in *The Victoria History of Norfolk* (1901), concluded that *Venta* was a small Roman country town. In the early years of this century, and prior to the excavations, it was appreciated that this was the centre for the Iceni and that their tribal council held its meetings in its basilica.

It was the morning of Friday 20th July 1928 which marked the most significant development in the study of the town. Arrangements had been made for an RAF aircraft to fly over the site and to take a series of aerial photographs. There had been exceptionally dry conditions that summer and conditions were perfect. The Roman street layout was picked out in spectacular detail within the whitened barley crop, enabling an accurate plan of the town to be drawn. Never before had this level of detail been visible to archaeologists and our understanding of the town was transformed in a single day.

The new details of the street plan and outlines of some major buildings provided the basic information from which the first excavations were planned. They aroused much interest and helped to generate the collection of funds for investigations of the site. An excavation committee was formed by the Norfolk and Norwich Archaeological Society, under their president Mr R.F.E. Ferrier. Excavations were planned and it was agreed that these should be undertaken by Donald Atkinson of Manchester University, who had recently completed similar work at the Roman town of Wroxeter. Work began in March, through to April, 1929 and then from June until August. They subsequently continued on an annual seasonal basis to 1935, with the single exception of 1932.

Our interpretation of *Venta* has been hindered because these excavations were never fully written-up or published. The excavation of 1929 was published in the journal *Norfolk Archaeology* in 1932. The work on the pottery kilns of 1930 was published in the *Journal of Roman Studies* in 1932. However, we are only left with brief annual reports of the subsequent work. Atkinson was still working on a final report of the site at the time of his death in 1963. Much later, in 1971, Professor Frere made use of the surviving excavation records to publish an account of the forum and baths, in the journal *Britannia*. An additional source has been the extra-mural work undertaken by Commander Mann, between 1932-7. His excavation of the Caistor Anglo-Saxon cemetery disturbed earlier Roman structures and refuse pits. More recently, information has come from work by metal-detector users, who have regularly reported their finds of artefacts and coins from extra-mural areas on all sides of the walled town.

The earliest settlement in the Tas Valley

The area around Caistor, centred on the confluence of the Rivers Yare and Wensum, is known to have been an important focus for settlement throughout prehistoric times. The Neolithic (4,500-2,200 BC) henge monument at Arminghall is situated just 1.5km to the north-east. Henge is the name given to circular enclosures which have banks outside their ditches. Here, a large circular bank 15m wide, with internal and external ditches, surrounded a central space of 27m in diameter. Within the central part, large timber uprights were arranged in a U-shaped formation. This site was constructed as a magnificent and visually impressive monument of great importance to the population of the region. There is also a concentration of round barrows, which were circular burial mounds constructed from the Middle Neolithic to the Bronze Age (from c2,700-c700BC) in the vicinity. Evidence of Iron Age (700BC-AD43) activity was found just 800m to the north, at Harford Farm, where six ritual or funerary enclosures were revealed during excavations between 1989-91, along the route of the Norwich Southern Bypass. Pottery of similar date was also found at Arminghall. This rich focus of prehistoric activity was probably associated with the joining of the Rivers Tas and Yare at that point.

There was also Iron Age occupation across the site of the Roman town. Evidence comes in the form of artefacts, especially metalwork finds, which are most durable. Such artefacts have regularly been reported to archaeologists by local metal-detector users, including numerous Icenian silver coins. La Tene style brooches and terrets, which are harness-rings made of bronze, have been discovered to the east and west of the town walls, as well as from the centre of the site. Coin and metalwork hoards in the vicinity serve to reinforce the importance of this area in the Late Iron Age period. This material dates both to the years before and after the Roman conquest of AD 43, right up to the rebellion of Boudica, in AD 61, the date of which marks the end of the Iron Age in this area.

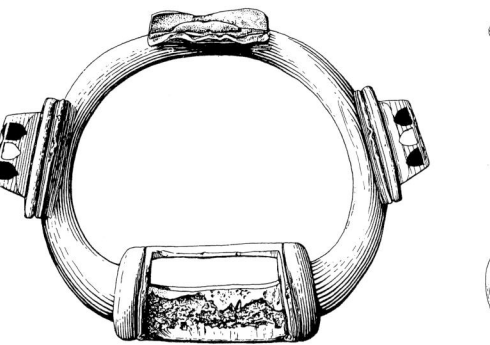

Iron Age terret (rein-ring). Scale 1:1

Who were the Iron Age people who inhabited this area? They spoke a Celtic language and were strongly religious people. Although the population was steadily increasing they did not inhabit towns. They were farmers and lived in round houses within their farmsteads. The Celts were flamboyant people as shown by their elaborate weapons and chariot fittings. They enhanced their personal appearance by the use of lavish personal dress ornaments, such as gold and silver torcs (neck rings). Today, we find evidence of their settlements in the form of pottery and these metalwork objects. Writing in the mid-first century BC, Julius Caesar mentions a tribal group living north of the Thames called the Cenimagni. These may have been the people later known to us as the Iceni. The name given by Caesar could possibly be interpreted as 'the Eceni Magni', which can in turn be translated as 'the Great Iceni'.

The Client Kingdom and its fall

Following the arrival of the Romans in AD 43, the land inhabited by the Iceni appears to have remained neutral during the main period of the conquest of Britain. Although not named, this may have been one of the eleven kingdoms whose submission was recorded on the triumphal arch of Claudius in Rome. The Roman historian Tacitus, who was writing between AD 75-120, indicates that the Iceni already regarded themselves as allies of Rome in AD 47, when the Romans were establishing a defence between the Severn and the Trent, known as the Fosse Way frontier. The Governor of Britain wanted to disarm all peoples living to the south of that line, which resulted in a revolt within the Iceni. This uprising was put down by auxiliary troops and the tribe was subsequently ruled over by King Prasutagus. Their land became what is known as a Client Kingdom, under which it retained most of its own laws and its independence, in return for recognising the supremacy of the Emperor.

Under this agreement, Prasutagus was expected to name the emperor as his heir. Unfortunately, he attempted to bequeath half of his estate to his family in his will. Upon his death, in AD 61, Catus Decianus the Procurator (Treasury officer) of Britain was sent to the kingdom in order to enforce Nero's authority and secure the whole of the estate for the Emperor. The Romans acted in an inflammatory manner and committed outrages which culminated in the violation of Boudica, wife of the dead king, and her two daughters. Simmering anger within the tribe ignited into rebellion and desire for revenge, under the leadership of Boudica.

Boudica has often been written as 'Boadicea', which was the Victorian translation. The version 'Boudicca', as used by Tacitus, is also sometimes used. However, the correct form should have only one c. The name derives from the Celtic *bouda*, which means victory (*buddog* in modern Welsh).

The Iceni poured south and were joined by the adjacent tribe, the Trinovantes (who inhabited the area now covered by Essex and parts of Suffolk, Hertfordshire and Cambridgeshire), before marching on the Roman capital at *Camulodunum* (Colchester). Britain was a new province and that town was still under construction and relatively defenceless. It was razed to the ground, followed by the new settlements at *Londinium* (London) and *Verulamium* (St. Albans). The Roman governor Paulinus eventually lured the Celtic army to battle at a site of his choosing near Mancetter, in the Midlands.

Tacitus tells us how the Roman forces used the terrain to their advantage. They stood their ground despite being heavily outnumbered and launched their javelins at the advancing British army with devastating effect before bursting forward in a wedge formation. The cavalry then broke up all remaining pockets of resistance. The Romans showed no mercy and Tacitus tells how even the women and baggage animals were slaughtered as they tried to flee, being boxed-in by the baggage train which blocked their escape. In the aftermath of this decisive action the Icenian territory came under full Roman rule.

Just what happened to Boudica remains a mystery and the subject of folklore. Suetonius failed to capture her and according to Tacitus she took poison rather than be taken back to a Roman triumph. Dio Cassius, writing over a century later, says that she died of a disease and that she received a grand and costly burial. However, her burial site has not been found.

Left: Boudica in her war chariot

Below left: Coin hoard buried during Boudica's revolt

Below right: Coin of King Prasutagus. Scale 4:1

Enter the Romans

In the years following the invasion of Britain in AD 43, Roman forts were constructed across East Anglia. In the area covered by modern Norfolk, they were established at Swanton Morley, Horstead, Threxton, Ashill, Saham Toney and Barton Bendish. There is also evidence of a military presence at the small town of Scole, on the Norfolk-Suffolk border. Some of these would have been built prior to the Boudican uprising, while others, such as Saham Toney, after that. It is not yet possible to provide very precise dating for all of them. The Romans often sited such forts adjacent to centres of local population.

At Caistor, artefacts recovered from the centre of the walled town confirm an early Roman military presence. These include such items as harness and tunic fittings, as well as coins of Claudius known to have been carried by soldiers in the army of occupation during the mid-first century. There is also imported Samian Ware pottery dating from the reign of the emperor Nero (54-68) which may have been used by military personnel, and also earlier Claudian (41-54) Samian Ware from east of the town. Pottery kilns of a similar date were also found immediately north and south of the north wall and south of the southern town ditch. These have been identified as a military kiln complex to supply the army stationed here.

Additional evidence of a military presence has come from aerial photography, which has revealed three ditches, running roughly parallel to, and outside, the line of the later town walls on the south and east sides. Excavation to the south of the town by the Norfolk Archaeological Unit in 1997 was unable to date these features closely. The inner ditch was found to be V-shaped, with a depth of two metres. It produced second century pottery from fills half way down. The middle ditch was shallower, at 1.3m, while the profile of the outer ditch was indistinct. These defences might have originally run up to the River Tas, on the west and north sides, forming a roughly square defensive enclosure. In those days the river was wider and

Items used by soldiers. Left to right: Harness pendant, coin (as), armour hook.
Below: scabbard mount. Scale 1:1

straighter than today. It seems probable that they were originally constructed as part of a military fortress of the pre-, or immediately post-, Boudican period. Triple-ditches were a feature of early military defended forts in this area. Similar ditches have been identified around the forts of Saham Toney and Swanton Morley in Norfolk, and Pakenham and Coddenham in Suffolk.

The area enclosed by the ditches is approximately that of a full-sized legionary fortress. The Roman army in Britain was severely stretched following the Boudican rebellion, and the campaign in Wales. Any legionary presence in Norfolk after Boudica is likely to have been short-lived. However, there would have been the necessity to keep a close watch on the defeated tribe. The temporary stationing of a legion may have been required to ensure the peaceful transition to full Roman administration. Fifteen kilometres further north, a temporary fort, or marching camp, of similar legionary size has also been identified at Horstead.

Aerial view, looking east, showing the military triple ditches south of the walls

Foundation of the Roman town

The reason why the Roman town was situated at Caistor St. Edmund has caused much interest and debate. The layout of the Roman town, including the main street grid, has been dated to around AD 70. But why did the Romans choose this particular spot over other locations in the region?

There were certainly some geographical advantages. At this point the River Tas was wide and deep enough to allow medium-sized boats to bring trade goods from coastal ports. It was also far enough up the Yare/Wensum river system to allow roads to cross it easily. As a route centre, it lay on gravel terraces away from the heavier claylands to the west and south, which would have been relatively impassable in wet weather. However, these reasons are not enough. The position of Norwich, later favoured for settlement in the Late Saxon period, had stronger geographical advantages. What was special about Caistor St. Edmund? The answer may be that this location was developed by the Romans because it had already been a focus of native settlement during the years of the Client Kingdom.

Following the Boudican revolt of AD 61, there would have been a transition from martial law to a completely civil administration. The decision to create the town was probably taken within a year or two after the revolt. A local council would have been formed, known as an *ordo*, which was a sort of town council. In order to serve on the *ordo* there was a minimum property requirement, and all of its members were given responsibilities for individual elements of the council's work. These included the maintenance of streets and water supplies.

The people who lived in Roman Britain included very few immigrants from the Mediterranean world. The population of *Venta* would have been mainly made-up from the local Icenian population and only supplemented by some others, including traders, from further afield.

Right across the Roman world rich citizens who sought positions on such councils acted as benefactors to towns, enhancing the splendour of their buildings and seeking to make them grander than those of their neighbours. In Britain there is less evidence for the great generosity shown in other provinces of the Empire. Buildings here were more utilitarian and there are fewer inscriptions telling us about the generosity of individual citizens. However, towns were provided with facilities which were considered essential for a civilized life within the Roman world.

So, *Venta Icenorum* became the local *civitas* capital, or county town. It was the biggest town in northern East Anglia, between the other such centres at *Camulodunum* (Colchester) *Ratae* (Leicester) and *Lindum* (Lincoln). The process of Romanisation through the construction of towns was a countrywide process in the later years of the first century.

The late town wall, showing flint construction with tile coursing

The early Roman town

When the initial street grid was laid out it was intended that the town would be of some considerable size. Judging from the extent of the grid visible on aerial photographs, it originally covered an area twice that later defined by the flint walls. When *Venta* was founded, the Tas ran from south-to-north in a much straighter line west. These may have been constructed earlier than the main street grid.

Whenever the Romans decided to build a new town, a team of surveyors, or *grammatici*, were appointed to undertake the work. Once the town limits were established, sacrifices were made to the gods before construction work started. The rectangular plan, bisected by two main streets which crossed at right angles in the centre, was typical of Roman towns. The town was

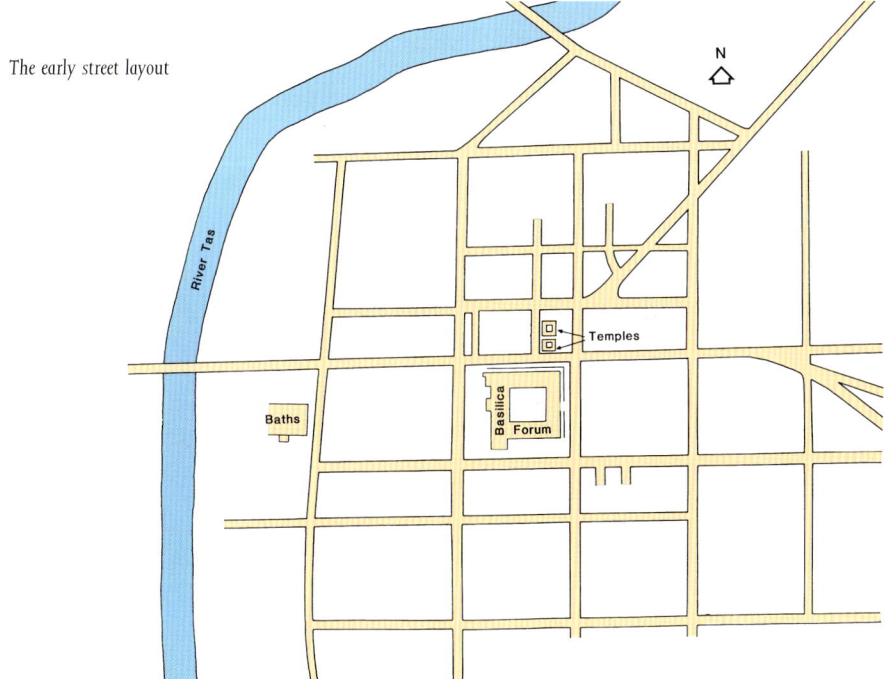

The early street layout

than today and it turned more sharply eastwards in the north. The town was located in an angle of the river. A rectilinear street grid was laid out, on a NNE/SSW alignment, the streets aligned quite closely with the original course of the Tas.

There are also streets which radiate from a nucleus just beyond the north-east corner of the walled area, which do not align with the main town grid. They run from a point now situated beneath the grounds of Caistor Hall to the north-west and south-

then divided into a neat grid of numbered blocks called *insulae*, which were separated by side-streets. The main public buildings were sited near the centre.

Roman roads and streets were constructed in a well-established manner. The road line was defined by ploughing outer ditches on either side. A central embankment was then prepared for the road proper. On top, a foundation of large stones, followed by smaller stones, were normally laid. The surface was cambered to allow efficient drainage. At *Venta*, a lower layer of ashen grey sand rested on the natural ground surface. Above the sand, successive layers of rammed-gravel, each of which became thicker towards the centre, gave a pronounced camber.

Dark lines can be seen on aerial photographs running down the centres of some streets and near the verges of others. These are the evidence for drains, originally constructed in timber, arranged to service the town.

The street layout was the only major development at *Venta* before 100 AD. There were no substantial buildings constructed during these early years, which would have been a very costly undertaking. Instead, the first buildings were more simple timber structures, while open spaces were left for the later addition of a forum and public baths, at the appropriate locations. It was not unusual for houses, shops and workshops in towns to be initially constructed in timber and later rebuilt in masonry when resources became available. The remains of simple wattle and daub houses were found in Insula IX, beneath later town houses.

Evidence for buildings of second century date was found due east of the walled town, during excavation of the Anglo-Saxon cemetery by Commander Mann. Unsubstantial timber, wattle and daub buildings, together with refuse pits and ancillary structures, building debris and pottery, were found beneath the whole area of the cemetery.

The major public buildings were the forum and baths, which were standard constructions at all Roman towns right across the Empire. Their plans varied to a certain extent. The elegance and size also varied according to the wealth of the local *ordo*, who had to finance the buildings. The forum at *Venta* lay in *Insula X*, approximately in the centre of the town, and it was originally built during the reign of the Emperor Hadrian (AD 117-38). It was replaced during the Antonine period (AD 138-80) and was later burnt down, probably early in the third century. It consisted of three sides of a square and was the town market place.

The first forum measured approximately 65m from the east colonnade to the rear wall of the basilica, in the west. The central courtyard measured 31.4m by 29.6m and was surrounded on three sides by a colonnade 6.1m wide in the north and south and 3.5m wide on the east side. In the centre of the square stalls were erected on market days. The entrance was from the east. The east range contained a row of

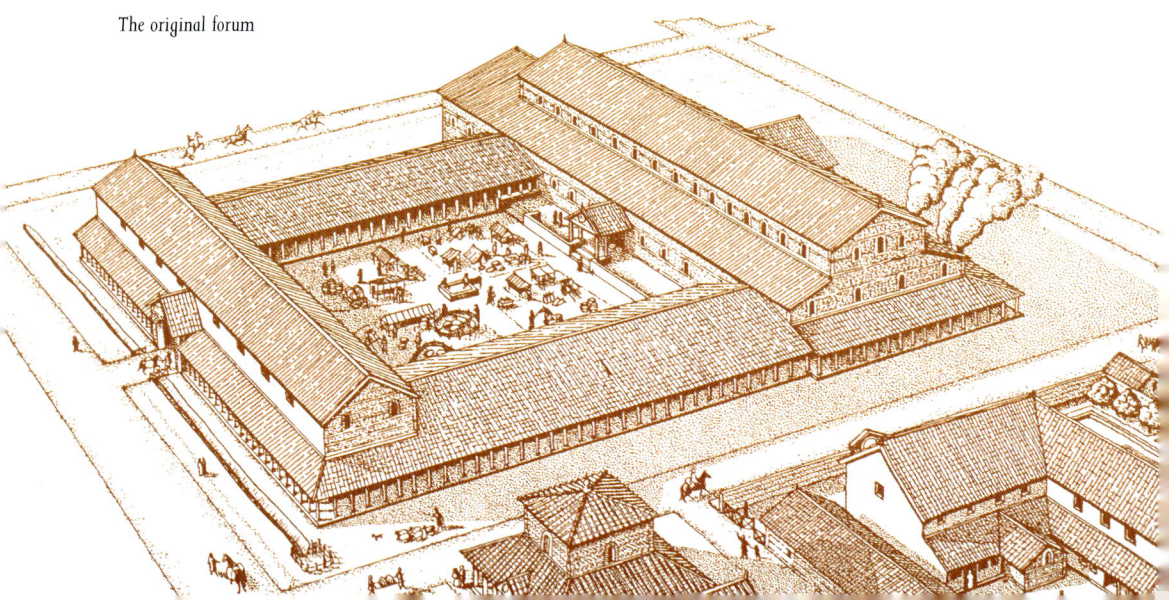

The original forum

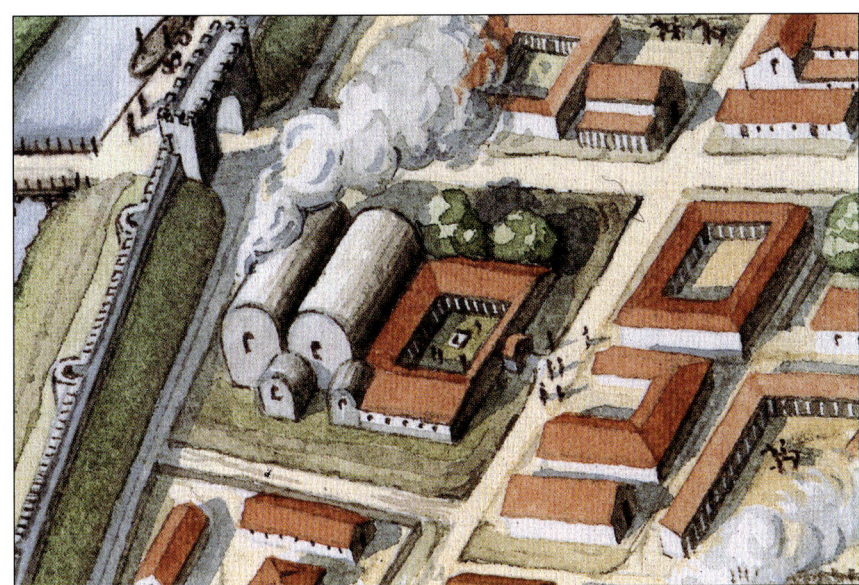

The baths, beside the River Tas

rooms on either side of the entrance passage. The north and south ranges consisted of long narrow halls. At the west end of the courtyard, three flights of tile steps led up to a narrow terrace in front of the basilica.

The basilica, or town hall, formed the west side of this range of buildings. It consisted of a nave, measuring 53.9 by 9.1m, internally with rooms projecting from the west and south walls. There were also two other offices beyond the north-west corner, which were warmed by channelled hypocausts. They were, no doubt, occupied by prominent members of the *ordo*.

Building costs within this complex were kept down by using brick and flint only for the main walls of the basilica and north wall of the forum. Elsewhere, there was a combination of chalk blocks and unfired clay bricks, which were set on flint sleeper walls.

We may compare the appearance of these prominent Roman buildings with the current arrangement of Norwich market and City Hall, from where civic dignitaries look out from their splendid offices across the assembled awnings of the market stalls covering the large piazza below.

The baths lay in *Insula XVII*, next to the river, to the west. They were excavated in 1935 but only a small part of the establishment was ever studied. This appears to have been built at the same date as the forum, during the Antonine period. No other people in European history were ever as clean as the Romans. Throughout their Empire, the inhabitants of towns went to great lengths to provide bathing facilities and these were often constructed with great elegance. It is a popular misconception that Roman Britain was inhabited by Italian immigrants. The population consisted of native peoples who were becoming 'Romanised' to a differing extent across the country. In Britain, bathing establishments tended to be less ostentatious but nonetheless became an essential part of daily life. Few town houses would have had their own private baths and the public baths acted as something of a social centre. They were centres of recreation for the town community.

Men and women were used to bathing together during the early years of the Empire but the Emperor Hadrian (117-38) forbade this practice. Thereafter, men and women would either use different sections of the same building or bathe at different times. But bathing was only part of the attraction of these establishments. Some were equipped with a gymnasium. After exercise, bodies were rubbed with olive oil, which was then scraped-off with a curved bronze hand-held instrument called a *strigil*. Masseurs were also in attendance. Following exercise they would bathe.

At *Venta*, people entered the baths from the street through a single entrance on the east side. This led into an open courtyard with columns on all sides, known as a peristyle. The surrounding porticos were floored with cement and there were three doorways leading into the *frigidarium*. This cold room ran the full width of the building. Beyond it lay the *tepidarium* (warm room) and a circular *laconicum* (heated room), enclosed within a square outer wall. To the north of the entrance was a

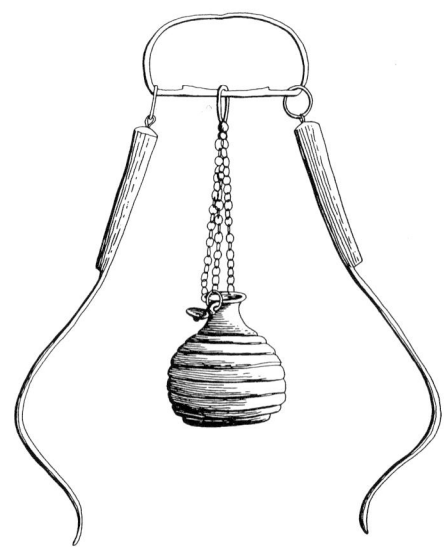

Strigils and oil bottle. Scale 1:3

rectangular room which may have been a dressing room or latrine. The scale of the baths suggests that they supported a barrel-vaulted roof.

Following the bathing, they would be rubbed-down by attendants and congregate in the vicinity, using this as a social focus, conversing with friends and listening to poetry recitals. Tradespeople and food sellers would use these places as prime locations for business. The Roman writer Seneca (c4BC-AD65) tells us how noisy an urban bathing establishment could be as a result of all this. He describes the noise generated by the cries of the confectioner and sausage dealer, as well as that from peddlers and cook stalls. Seneca also describes the piercing screams from the clients of yet another regular occupant of the establishment, the hair plucker!

The constant threat of fire must have been as great a hazard in Roman towns as it undoubtedly was in medieval times, particularly with the extensive use of wood for construction. Like the forum, the baths at *Venta Icenorum* were ravaged by fire and then reconstructed towards the end of the second century.

The Romans ensured the supply of fresh water to their towns by building a reservoir, distribution tanks and walled conduits. There is evidence of such a water supply and sewage system at *Venta*. A section of wooden water pipe has been recovered during excavation and the locations of drains and sewers can be seen running along the streets in aerial photographs. It is noticeable how the western half of the town falls away towards the River Tas, providing natural drainage. The town may also have been served by a supply of running water from an aqueduct, which could have led to the site from higher ground, to the east. Public baths tended to require both aqueducts and drains but the former constructions often escape identification because their remains, if any, are slight. The river was ultimately the recipient of the town waste, from the drainage and sewage system.

Industry and trade

The earliest industry to be recorded from *Venta Icenorum* was the early military period pottery production. Four kilns were excavated which appear to have been geared to supplying the requirements of the garrison. Their products were Romanised versions of early cooking pots and bowls, as used by Late Iron Age people. It is thought that the potters who worked these *Venta* kilns were immigrants who came across with the Romans, or native workers trained in Roman craft techniques. They operated between the reign of the emperor Nero and the early years of Vespasian (54-70). When the town streets were laid out these kilns were abandoned. Their remains were flattened and spread to level the site. This then became mixed with later material in the infilling of pits at the stage of the first organised urban development of the site.

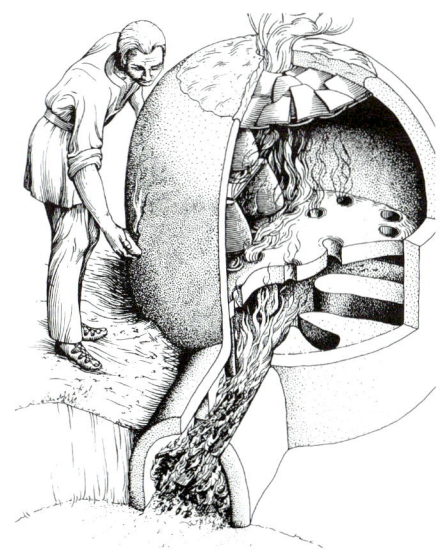

Kiln during use

As *Venta Icenorum* developed, commerce played an important role in the everyday life of the Roman town. Local and long distance trade provided the main activity at this centre of population in the heart of the region.

Activity at the town was principally geared to local agriculture and particularly to sheep farming. Organised agriculture was practised in the surrounding countryside, while the processing and export of woollen goods was a major industry in the town. This is reflected in the finds - a large iron wool comb was discovered during excavations, as well as spindle whorls, iron shears and leather-working needles. Carbonised cereal grain has also been found on the site.

Pot containing carbonised grain

In *Insula IX*, to the north of the forum, a glass manufacturing workshop, probably for window glass, was constructed around AD 300 by re-building two earlier town houses at this location. A bronze-working furnace was also discovered in the vicinity of Caistor Hall, to the north-east.

Venta was a route centre situated at the hub of regional traffic. Roads connected the site with the fenland in the west, which was an area of agricultural importance and focus of salt production, and the small town of Brampton in the north, which had a major pottery industry. A road to the west, which preceded the route of the modern A140, ran due south through the small town of Scole and on to

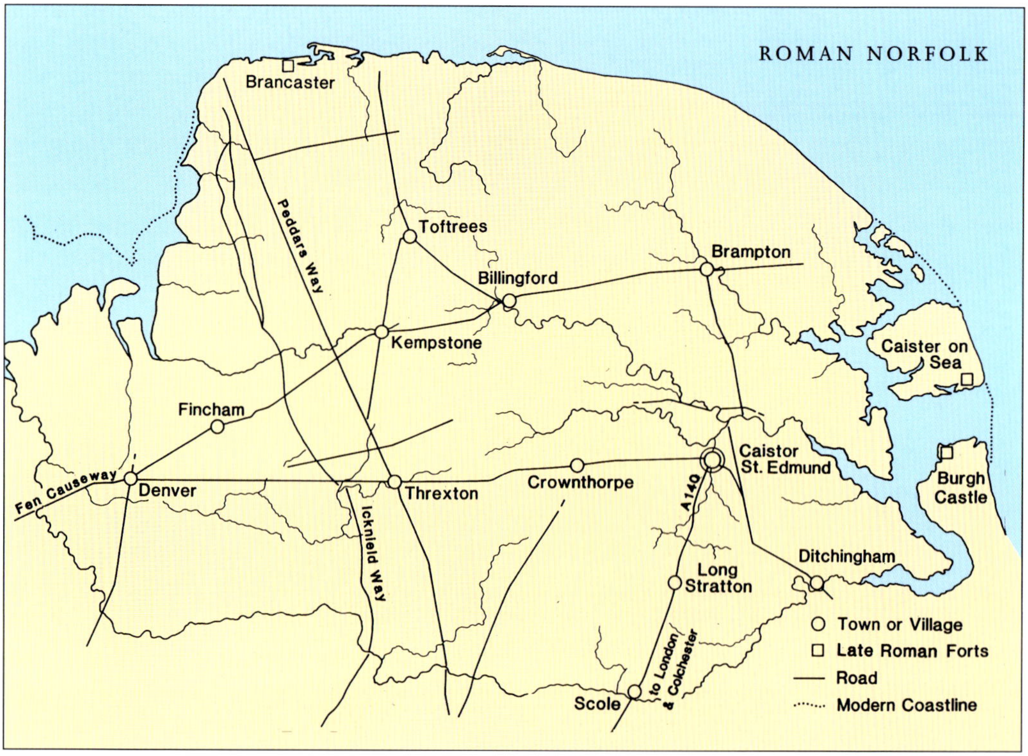

ROMAN NORFOLK

Colchester. By river, the town was connected to a great estuary, which covered the area occupied today by the marshes between Acle and Great Yarmouth. Other sites adjacent to the River Yare are suggest-

Gemstone, showing a ship and lighthouse. Scale 4:1

ed by the presence of timbers, at Brundall and at Trowse. By this route, agricultural produce was transported to coastal ports for transfer to larger sea-going craft and subsequent trading with markets along the eastern seaboard of Britain and the Continent. This transhipment may have taken place at the Roman forts at Caister-on-Sea and Burgh Castle, which were strategically located at the entranceway to the estuary from the North Sea. Products imported from abroad, coming to Caistor by way of the same route, include the fine red glazed pottery known as Samian ware, and Argonne ware, which both came from Gaul (France). Trade with Germany is shown by the presence of Rhenish and Mayen wares.

Remains of timbers and substantial iron fittings have been described and found adjacent to the river, in the location where a wharf once existed. This would have allowed craft to moor between the west gate and north-west corner of the wall. The original bend of the river in this stretch explains the corresponding, slightly curved, shape of the west wall of the town.

Everyday life in the town

We cannot be certain how many people lived at *Venta Icenorum*. We do not yet know the full area covered by the town at its greatest extent. Until this is defined and further excavation is undertaken to reveal the density of domestic housing, this must remain speculation. Herculaneum, a Roman town of 22 hectares in southern Italy, is thought to have had a population of four to five thousand. Archaeologists have estimated that between five and ten thousand lived at Colchester during the first century AD. On this comparative basis, *Venta* in its later walled stage may have contained perhaps three thousand, while the earlier, unwalled, town could have had a population of four to five thousand.

Two town houses were excavated to the north of the forum, in *Insula IX*, next to two Romano-Celtic temples. Building 1 was a long narrow structure aligned north-south. Building 2 was separated by a narrow space

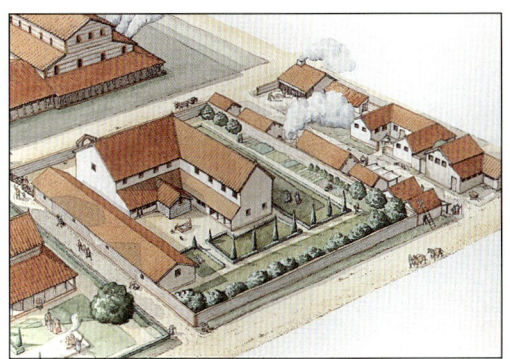

A town house, north of the forum

and formed an L-shape. Excavation revealed more details of this second structure, showing it to have been built of flint and mortar. The internal walls and partitions were decorated with painted plaster. In the main corridor, this consisted of horizontal bands of red and dark brown or black, separated by narrow white lines. These panels also carried more intricate decoration, including floral patterns. Windows of the house were filled with a greenish glass. Just a few small stone cubes used in mosaics, known as *tesserae*, were found in the west range and suggest at least one decorated floor. The floors of both buildings were mainly concrete and the houses were surrounded by gravel pavements.

These houses were probably built in the early third century. Then, possibly around AD 300, they were united and in the area originally occupied by the north end of building 1, a number of furnaces and hearths were constructed. This became a workshop for the manufacture of window glass until around the middle of the fourth century.

Another house was investigated further north, in *Insula VII*, which had been built above earlier pottery kilns. This was of substantial construction but had wattle and daub walls. There was a range of rooms, with external corridors and an apse at the east end. There was also a small private bath suite. Elsewhere, the lower classes and artisans would have lived in smaller houses close to their places of work. This was often in apartments situated above or behind workshops and shops.

The region suffers from a lack of stone and it was necessary to find alternative construction materials. Flints were used in the footings of some structures. Other domestic buildings may have been made more simply from brick, wood and wattle and daub, while roofs were made from tiles. During the excavation of an Anglo-Saxon cemetery between 1932-37, situated just 300m to the east of the town wall, some Roman masonry and timber structures were identified. Signs of wealth among the inhabitants are apparent, with the discovery of mosaics from some buildings. This form of flooring is not commonly found within Norfolk, although some

A domestic table setting

and tables, covered by awnings, set up within the market place.

Adjacent to the river, businessmen would have constructed store-houses to receive consignments of goods being moved in and out by boat. Such imports would have included large pottery transport and storage vessels known as amphorae, which contained wine, to be sold-on to stallholders and inns in the town.

Oil lamp and tableware

may have been lost through ploughing in more recent years.

The town was a focus of trading activity, the streets lined with shops selling an array of goods. Perishable foodstuffs grown in market gardens around the town boundaries were brought in daily by pack animals and carts. Behind shopfronts there were workshops, where shopkeepers sat at the counter. A row of shops can be seen on aerial photos, along the east-west street outside the south wall. A rich variety of wares for sale would have lined the streets, including baking, clothing, carpentry, leathergoods and jewellery. Livestock, too, were brought to the town for sale. Foodstuffs were also sold on market stalls

Other Roman ways of life are revealed by finds from the town. Iron *styli* were used for writing on wax tablets. Scalpels have been found, showing the presence of Roman medical practices. Large numbers of bronze and silver coins from the site reflect the daily trading activity carried out at this bustling settlement.

Wax tablet and styli used for writing. Scale 1:3

Recreation

An amphitheatre has been identified by aerial photography to the south of the town. From the ground, it is only visible by the presence of a slight dip in the surface. This would have been the main focus of recreation for the town's population and

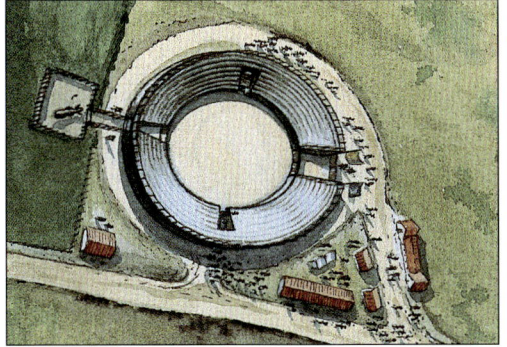

The amphitheatre

for the surrounding area. It is located 90m to the south of the walls and shows as an oval cropmark, with its long axis aligned north-to-south. Although not excavated, further evidence of the plan has been revealed by geophysical survey. It was a stone, masonry or brick construction. The dimensions of the oval arena have been measured as 40m x 33m. There was a south gateway but no such opening has been located in the north. The outlines of rooms surrounding the arena, positioned beneath the seating banks, have been traced.

Decorated glass cup, depicting a chariot race. Scale 1:2

Tiers of seats were built around the central arena. The audience was protected from events by a high wall. In contrast to theatres, amphitheatres were used for more spectacular forms of entertainment, including wild animal shows and gladiatorial battles. The army also used them for exercises and parades. On show days, the road leading to the amphitheatre would have been lined with stalls selling prepared foodstuffs and souvenirs.

Everyday recreations in Roman Britain included gambling and games of chance. Six-sided dice are commonly found on settlements and counters for board games have been found at *Venta*. Playing surfaces could vary from beautiful inlaid tables and carved wooden boards to grids scratched in public places.

A board game, with counters

Religion and burials

For rich and poor alike, religion played an important part of everyday life in the Roman world, as it had within society in the years before Roman rule. Local Celtic gods became associated with their Roman counterparts, making the acceptance of Roman religion much easier. The resulting mixture can be called 'Romano-Celtic'.

A divine force was considered to be everywhere, in woods, streams and in the household. Respect to the gods played a major role in all activities. Numerous objects associated with this religious behaviour have been found at *Venta Icenorum*. The cult of Mercury is shown by the figurine of this deity, who is also depicted on the handle of a pan. Other figurines and miniatures were used as cult objects, including an eagle, cockerel, axe and an arrangement of three linked vases. On the bank of the river was found a lead *defixio*, or curse tablet, dedicated to the God Neptune. This had been tightly rolled-up and inscribed on one side. This requests the help of Neptune to seek out a thief and recover a list of stolen items, including a wreath, bracelets, a cap, a mirror, a head-dress, a pair of leggings and ten pewter vessels. This discovery associated with the Sea God further highlights the importance attached to the role of river by the town's inhabitants and to continental trade across the North Sea.

Two temples lie in *Insula IX*, immediately north of the forum. Romano-Celtic temples such as these consisted of a square central building (the cella), surrounded by a concentric wall, which created an ambulatory, or walk-way. These examples are very similar in size and shape. The one closer to the forum had thicker walls and could have supported a more substantial superstructure. Both were built during the later second century but we are not certain whether they were in fact both in use at the same time. Neither do we know which gods were associated with them.

Another temple complex is known outside the walled area, to the north-east of Caistor Hall. The temple again had a square plan and lay within an outer wall, which defined the sacred area or *temenos*. This temple has been known since 1932 and was excavated between 1950 and 1957. The complex was entered through a monumental gateway in the west. A large ancillary building was located in the north east of the enclosure and a smaller structure also lay to the west. The temple itself had a walk-way between its inner and outer walls and its floor was laid with *tesserae*. Two altar bases were found during excavation. Surface finds have shown that this temple saw its main use in the years before AD 200.

We have very little evidence for the cemeteries which usually define the limits of a Roman town. These may have lined the sides of roads beyond the town, as was required by law. During the nineteenth century a rectangular flint structure was located to the north-east of the town walls and this may have been a walled funerary enclosure.

Above: The two temples.
Inset: Pan handle, depicting the god Mercury. Scale 1:3

The late Roman town

Wall-building was begun around towns across Britain during the first half of the third century, possibly during the reign of the Emperor Caracalla (198-217). By the 270s, a further massive programme of town wall construction had covered Roman Britain. The walls around *Venta* belong to this later period of construction. These walls, made of stone and flint, replaced earlier earthwork defences at many towns.

When *Venta's* walls were constructed, the town was reduced in size by about a half, to 14 hectares. A similar reduction in size occurred elsewhere, at sites such as Silchester and Canterbury. Although not dated archaeologically, it is likely that *Venta's* walls were built during the early 270s. Consolidation of the north wall between 1987-89 allowed a small scale programme of recording, which gave an insight into their construction and full dimensions.

The north wall originally stood to a height of 7.0m above ground level. It was approximately 4.0m thick and was topped with a parapet and walkway. The inner face was covered by an earthen rampart, which still survives, forming a 25 degree slope. The wall was constructed using three levels of tile coursing. The inner and outer faces were built-up using dressed flint and the core of the wall was infilled at intervals. Beyond the wall on the south and east sides was a berm or ledge, between its base and the ditch, of approximately 4.6m. The single ditch, measured 24m wide and 5.2m deep.

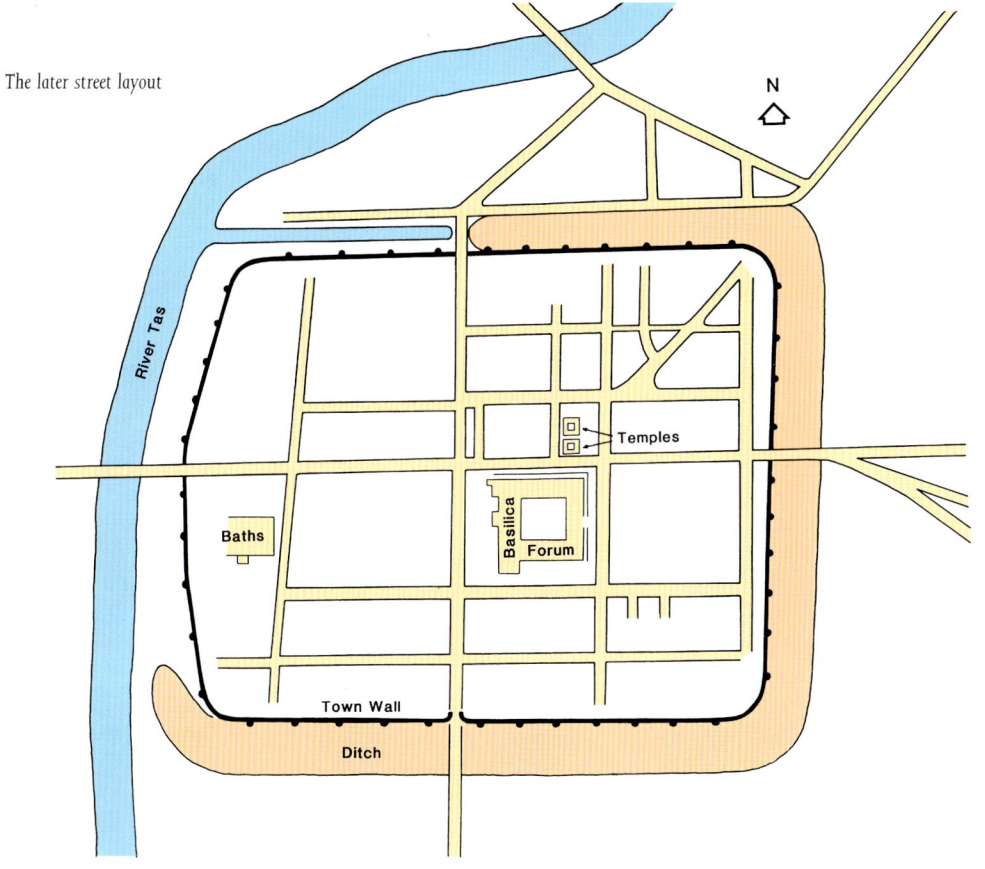

The later street layout

Today, the western half of the north wall is visibly narrower than the eastern half. Although this section may have been more severely robbed of its flint in post-Roman centuries, the surviving masonry is remarkably slighter than the adjacent magnificent stretch of wall to the east of the north gate. Such a marked difference may indicate that the western section was originally constructed in a less substantial fashion. It is possible that an artificial channel from the River Tas was cut just outside this stretch of wall, allowing small boats to moor alongside. This would explain why the wall did not need to be as strong in this sector.

There was a single gateway situated in the centre of each wall. The southern gateway, excavated by Atkinson, consisted of a single opening 4m wide, set between curved inturns of the curtain wall. The entrance passage was 4m deep with arches at each end and socket holes for double doors in the masonry. There would have been a single tower over the entrance. There were square guardrooms on each side, which were entered from the rampart sides.

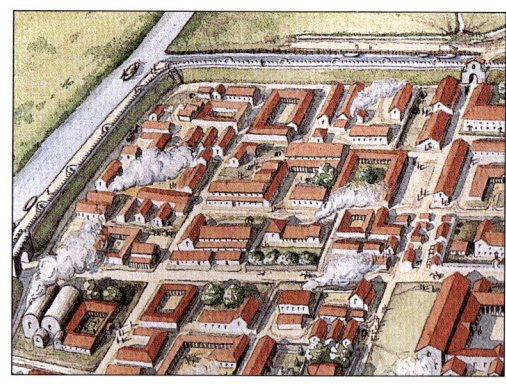
The north west sector, showing the river and channel

The south gateway

One of the more remarkable features of the town wall is in the addition of its bastions. These were additional fortifications

The north wall during consolidation work in 1989

projecting from the face of the wall. Two shapes of bastion have been identified at *Venta*, which are rectangular and semi-circular. This is the only town in Britain known to have been given two different forms of bastion. It may be that one type was contemporary with the wall construction and that the others were later additions, perhaps replacing the earlier form. Atkinson showed their frequency to have been seven U-shaped and six rectangular-shaped examples between the south gate and south east corner, positioned alternately. One U-shaped bastion has survived well and is located by the west gate.

The later forum

Late in the second or in the early third century part of the town, including the forum and baths, was badly damaged by fire. Timber buildings beyond the eastern wall of the forum had already been destroyed by fire, which appeared to be at the end of the second century. The forum remained derelict for a long period, not being rebuilt until towards the end of the third century. The second forum was a smaller and simpler structure, using little of the wall positions of its predecessor. The internal courtyard measured 29.6m north to south and lacked both the range of rooms in the east and the long halls in the north and south ranges. In the east, there were merely internal and external porticos, backed by single rooms north and south. On the north and south sides, central rooms projected back from single porticos.

The earlier steps leading up to the basilica were now covered by a gravel ramp. Excavations did not reveal evidence for a new basilica after the fire but this may have been removed by later plough damage to the site. Whether such a new building occupied the same position, or whether remaining features of the earlier basilica were re-used, is impossible to say.

The south gateway during excavation

The end of the Roman town

The authority of the Roman Empire began to break down from the 340s AD. The ultimate fate of the town and its inhabitants are shrouded in uncertainty. Atkinson discovered remains of human bodies, which he interpreted as evidence for a massacre of the town's inhabitants by Saxon mercenary troops. However, it is more likely that these skeletons originated from one of the nearby cemeteries. Certainly, coin evidence shows that occupation continued within the town walls into the early years of the fifth century but it is uncertain just how long it survived beyond this. No evidence for Saxon settlement has been found within the area. However, there is plentiful evidence for the presence of continuing Saxon occupation right across the surrounding landscape.

An Anglo-Saxon cemetery was located on a hill, just 350m to the east of the town walls. Three hundred and seventy-six cremations and sixty inhumation burials were discovered during excavations undertaken between 1932-7. Several hundred burial urns were recovered (a small number of

An Anglo-Saxon burial urn. Scale 1:4

which were Roman pots). Here it was that an early Anglian chieftain established himself. His followers continued to live at, and to be buried at, the same location. The cemetery continued in use throughout the fifth century and beyond. Towards the end of its life, there was a change in burial custom to inhumation. This may have coincided with a conversion from paganism to Christianity within the community. A second Anglo-Saxon cemetery lies just 300m to the north of the walled town, at Markshall, which was in use by the middle of the fifth century. Between 1989-91 a third Anglo-Saxon cemetery was excavated on the route of the Norwich southern bypass, at Harford Farm, just 800m to the north of *Venta*. The final phase of inhumation burials at these sites suggests the existence of a local community around the former Roman town which continued at least as late as the sixth century and probably into the seventh.

Over thirty coins of Middle Saxon date have been found mainly to the west of the town but also to the north and south. These indicate a continued presence across the area through the seventh, eighth and ninth centuries. This continuity of settlement must have been related in some respect to the enclosed site of the former Roman town, which provided an even more highly visible focus in the landscape than it does today. But just what role did it play at that time? Barbara Green and D.M. Metcalf have suggested that a reason for the absence of any post-Roman finds from inside the town may be related to the presence of the church located in its south-east corner. It is possible that there may have been an earlier church on the same site, and that the walled enclosure belonged to a monastic foundation, accounting for the otherwise strange absence of coin finds from that area alone.

The accumulated evidence now points to a continuation of settlement at Caistor in the post-Roman period, focused on the site of the late Roman walled town. In this way, Caistor remained a prominent regional centre until it was superceded by Norwich during the ninth and tenth centuries.

The Church of St Edmund

The church, situated in the south-east corner of the walled town, is a prominent feature of the site today. Its ground plan fits well into the Roman street pattern and it is possible that this arrangement represents continuity from earlier churches founded in late Roman times, when the streets were still in use, and continuing through the Saxon period. No other post-Roman structures are known to have been constructed on the site.

The nave dates from the reign of King Edward the Confessor (1042-66). Edward gave the church to the Abbey of Bury St. Edmunds, an act which accounts for the dedication of the church and of the village to St Edmund. The chancel was constructed c1300. The west tower is unbuttressed. It has brick bell-openings and battlements panelled in brick and flint.

Inside, an octagonal stone font dates from between 1402 and 1419. It is highly decorated with four lions and four angels, with signs of the four evangelists against the bowl. It also carries the arms of Edward the Confessor and St. Edmund.

It is not unusual for churches to be built inside the walls of Roman towns. Others which are found in similar peripheral locations within town walls are at Silchester and Wroxeter, both of which similarly remained devoid of other post-Roman construction. Elsewhere, where the sites underwent a revival, they often occupied a more prominent position in relation to the former town layout, as at Lincoln. Early churches are also known from inside the walls of Saxon Shore forts, as at Burgh Castle, Bradwell-on-Sea (Essex), Reculver (Kent) and Portchester (Hampshire).

Above: The font

Left: The church

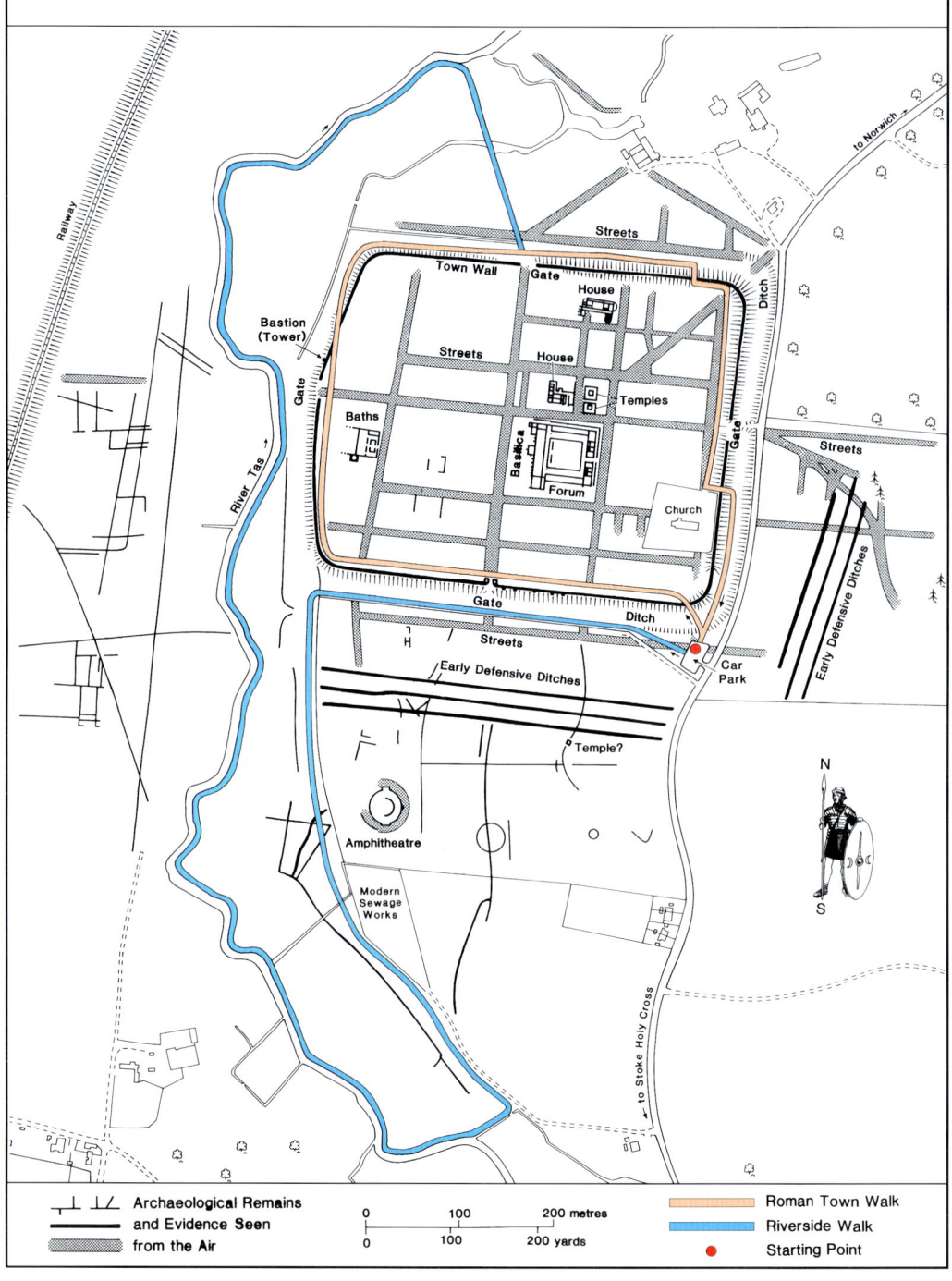

The site within its landscape

Venta Icenorum is situated within a rich historic landscape. The Roman town can best be viewed from the raised positions of the A140(T) Ipswich Road and from the main London to Norwich railway line. At certain times of the year, particularly during dry months and in snowy conditions, the Roman street grid can be seen very clearly.

The locations of other former sites are visible from the town itself. Just to the east, an Early Saxon cemetery was located. On raised ground to the north, at Harford Farm, an Iron Age burial site and Saxon cemetery have both been excavated. To the northeast, the prehistoric site of Arminghall Henge is situated, which is a ditched and banked enclosure of Neolithic date.

Tour of the Site

The site of Caistor St. Edmund is now owned and managed by the Norfolk Archaeological Trust, who acquired the land in order to protect the site and its setting for posterity. Archaeological layers are now safeguarded from damage and the whole site has been established as an area in which native flora and wildlife can flourish.

There are two signposted walks. One leads visitors around the Roman defences and has a series of interpretation panels, with aerial photographs and reconstruction paintings, explaining the history of the town. The other longer, riverside, walk follows the River Tas, allowing visitors to enjoy the wildlife and natural habitats.

Finds from the Site

The finds from the excavations at Venta Icenorum are now in the care of the Norfolk Museums and Archaeology Service. Many of these can now be seen in the new archaeology displays at Norwich Castle Museum.

Further reading

Publications relating to excavations at Caistor St Edmund are:
D. Atkinson 1930, 'Caistor Excavations', *Norfolk Archaeology* 24, 93-139.
D. Atkinson 1932, 'Three Caistor pottery kilns', *Journal of Roman Studies* 22, 35-46.
D. Atkinson 1935, 'Roman pottery from Caistor-next-Norwich', *Norfolk Archaeology* 26, 197-230.
M.J. Darling 1987, 'The Caistor-by-Norwich "massacre" reconsidered', *Britannia* 18, 263-72.
J.A. Davies 1992, 'Excavations of the north wall, Caistor St. Edmund, 1987-89', *Norfolk Archaeology* 41 pt. 3, 325-37.
S.S. Frere 1971, 'The forum and baths of Caistor-by-Norwich', *Britannia* 2, 1-26.
D. Gurney 1986, 'A Romano-Celtic temple site at Caistor St. Edmund', in 'Excavations at Thornham, Warham, Wighton and Caistor St. Edmund, Norfolk', *East Anglian Archaeology* 30, 37-58.
J.N.L. Myres and B. Green 1973, 'The Anglo-Saxon cemeteries of Caistor-by-Norwich and Markshall, Norfolk', *Report of the Research Committee of the Society of Antiquaries London* 30.

For the Boudican uprising:
P. Sealey 1997, *The Boudican Revolt Against Rome* (Shire).
G. Webster 1978, *Boudica: the British Revolt Against Rome AD 60*, 2nd edn (Batsford).

For Roman Norfolk and Suffolk:
J.A. Davies 1996, 'The Iron Age and Roman periods', in *A Festival of Norfolk Archaeology* (Norfolk and Norwich Archaeological Society), 21-29.
D. Gurney 1996, 'The 'Saxon Shore' in Norfolk', in *A Festival of Norfolk Arhcaeology* (Norfolk and Norwich Archaeological Society), 30-39.
I.E. Moore, J. Plouviez and S. West 1988, *The Archaeology of Roman Suffolk* (Suffolk County Council).
B. Robinson and A. Gregory 1987, *Celtic Fire and Roman Rule* (Poppyland).

For Roman Britain:
S.S. Frere 1987, *Britannia: a history of Roman Britain* (3rd edition, Routledge and Kegan Paul).
M. Millett 1995, *Roman Britain* (Batsford/English Heritage).
T.W. Potter and C. Johns 1992, *Roman Britain* (British Museum).
P. Salway 1981, *Roman Britain* (Clarendon Press).

ISBN 0-9540676-0-6